REACHING THE CHILD WITH AUTISM THROUGH ART

Practical, "fun" activities to enchance motor skills
and improve tactile and concept awareness

by

Toni Flowers, B.S., M.S., Ed. Specialist

Future Horizons, Inc.
721 W. Abram St.
Arlington, Texas 76013

800-489-0727
817-277-0727
817-277-2270 (fax)

Website: www.FutureHorizons-autism.com
E-mail: info@FutureHorizons-autism.com

ISBN# 1-885477-23-6

TABLE OF CONTENTS

Too often children with autism are "left out" of art class because they are difficult to reach. The experiences in the Artistic Autistic have been "Autism Tested" and given the "lick, sniff, twiddle" seal of approval by children with autism everywhere.

INTRODUCTION

Art is a feeling, an aura, a pleasant memory.

Art is an expression of self. A state of mind. An act not always recorded.

There should be no failure in art — only the release of creativity.

All children benefit from art, but children with autism in particular, who may experience some or all of the following:

1. Delayed and/or disturbed physical, social, and language skills;

2. Abnormal responses to sensations affecting one sense or a combination of senses or responses: sight, hearing, touch, balance, smell, taste, reaction to pain, and the way the child holds his or her body;

3. Absent or delayed speech and language, despite normal thinking capabilities;

4. Abnormal manner of relating to people, objects, and events;

— Autism Society of America

can benefit from the creativity and good feelings art produces.

Art leads the child in a positive direction.
Art helps in the development of a positive self image.

Art also helps to develop —

figure ground discrimination	directionality
concept development	cause and effect
spatial relationships	body in space
form discrimination	perceptual motor skills
sequencing	tactile / kinesthetic awareness
fine motor skills	attention span
eye contact	pride in accomplishment
and an appreciation of beauty in the environment	

Art as I perceive it does not always result in "something to take home". When there is a finished product, it is for the pride of both the parent and child. The act of doing is for the enjoyment and development of the child alone.

While in college, I was fortunate enough to have an art instructor who did something all the students thought radical. He took away the brushes and canvas and made us use everyday objects in the creation of our art work. There was resistance from the students at first. Then we started having fun.

1

There was competition to see who could create the ugliest piece. I won. I concocted a collage of cooked and uncooked popcorn, paint, and plastic bubbles on a background of fungus ridden wood.

My mother, however, thought this was a beautiful piece of art. She displayed it proudly in her living room. When her house burned, and the picture with it, you would have thought she had lost a masterpiece. (When there is a finished product, it is for the pride of the parent.)

Although the class set out to outdo each other in grossness, something strange happened. This approach to art released such a creative surge that I went on to make some hauntingly beautiful pieces using pictures of my grandmother's birthplace, string, sandpaper and paint.

I got an "A" in the course, but I'll never forget the professor's comments as he surveyed my work. He said, "I don't know if this is the biggest collection of trash I've ever witnessed, or if it is the birth of artistic genius."

I don't think this teacher knew the full impact of what he taught me. Trash or artistic genius didn't matter. The enjoyment and growth I experienced in that course changed the way I looked at the world around me. I began questioning and I began trusting my abilities and instincts instead of reaching for comfortable truths.

I have been teaching since 1968. I have taught every grade from Kindergarten through College. I have worked with children labeled autistic, normal, physically handicapped, emotionally or behaviorally disturbed, learning disabled, visually or hearing impaired, academically talented, developmentally delayed, neurologically impaired, attention deficit disorder, with various and sundry syndromes, and all combinations thereof.

I have found art to be a valuable component of any child's education because they are all children first and foremost — not labels. *Always teach to the child's ability not their disability.*

Experiencing art should lead to an unfolding awareness of self and the environment.

To grow,

to expand,

to begin building trust within yourself,

and to have fun doing it,

to me, that is art!

CHOICES

Being the cause of changes in the environment is exciting. Being in control of these changes is a powerful experience for a child. The child should be as totally involved in each experience as possible, from selecting the medium, implement, and surface, to choosing colors and helping in any gathering or preparation. Some children are ready and able to make decisions and others are not. This should be left to the individuals involved. Some children jump right in, some have to be prodded, and still others need guidance from beginning to end.

The surface on which one creates does not always have to be paper, although paper certainly has its place in art experiences.

The implement used to get the medium on the surface does not always have to be a brush.

The medium does not always have to be paint.

The texture, the surface, the color, the size, all contribute to the uniqueness of the project.

The same experience can be reproduced on different surfaces, using different implements, and different mediums and turn out startlingly different.

While going through the list of choices, keep in mind that traditionally

the medium is *paint,*

the implement is a *brush,*

and the surface is *paper.*

Translate paint, brush, paper to Collage Experience #5 on page 15:

Medium	Egg shells and glue	Paint
Implement	Plastic bags and hands	Brush
Surface	Cardboard	Paper

Translate paint, brush, paper to Collage Experience #7 on page 17:

Medium	Water colors and soap	Paint
Implement	Brush	Brush
Surface	Face and mirror	Paper

Translate paint, brush, paper to Collage Experience #2 on page 12:

Medium	Tissue paper	Paint
Implement	Hands	Brush
Surface	Air	Paper

Translate paint, brush, paper to Collage Experience #9 on page 19:

Medium	Self-hardening clay	Paint
Implement	Hands	Brush
Surface	None required	Paper

DON'T LIMIT YOURSELF to one medium, surface or implement. Some implements, surfaces and mediums are interchangeable. An implement can become a surface. For example: a piece of carpet can be an implement to apply paint to the surface, burlap. Or, the burlap can become the implement to apply paint to the surface, carpet. The medium of sand can become the surface sand.

The experiences in this book are ones I have done in my various classes over the years.
Use these as a starting point, but don't stop there.

> Ransack the kitchen,
> the basement,
> the attic,
> and the garage.
>
> Look in hardware stores,
> department stores,
> grocery stores,
> drug stores,
> and peruse garage sales
> and thrift shops.

Keep an open mind and be creative.
Trust yourself and start your students on the road to trusting themselves!!!

DEFINITIONS

Collage • Painting • Play • Sculpture

COLLAGE   The combination of medium(s) on a surface with an adhering implement(s).   May result in a finished product.

PAINTING   A free or controlled movement of wet medium(s) over a surface with implement(s).   May result in a finished product.

PLAY   Manipulation of objects or movement of all or part of the body. Does not result in a finished product.

SCULPTURE   Three dimensional, free standing objects not requiring a surface. May result in a finished product.

COLLAGE EXPERIENCES
17 Experiences

Author's Note:

CAUTION when using strong glue. Closely supervise its use. Sometimes it is the only thing that will hold a project together but it must be kept off skin and away from eyes and mouths!!

CHOICES FOR COLLAGES

MEDIUM	IMPLEMENT	SURFACE
cotton balls	white school glue	cardboard tubes
rice	strong glue	cloth
sponges	plastic bag	velvet - felt
cloth	sponge	burlap
velvet - felt	water	fake fur
burlap	tongue	real fur
fake fur		lace
real fur		vinyl
lace		corduroy
vinyl		terry cloth
corduroy		leather
terry cloth		denim
leather		canvas
denim		gauze
canvas		ribbon
gauze		cardboard – flat
buttons		wood
bolts		foam plates
nuts		wallpaper
screws		contact paper
feathers		paper
popcorn		bark
beans		
rice		
newspaper		
pasta		
aluminum foil		
wax paper		
plastic wrap		
sandpaper		
paper plate		
paper cup		
paper napkin		
plastic fork		
plastic knife		
plastic spoon		
egg shells		
stickers		
flat rocks		
rope		
string		
yarn		
weeds		
flowers		
pebbles		
sticks		

COLLAGE EXPERIENCE #1

OBJECTIVES

Tactile/Kinesthetic Awareness
Fine Motor

CHOICES

MEDIUM (S)	IMPLEMENT (S)	SURFACE (S)
Dried weeds	Strong glue	Bark – good sized pieces
Dried flowers		
Pebbles		
Sticks, etc.		
String		
Pine Cones		

SUGGESTED DIRECTIONS

After you have gathered your materials and let them dry, arrange them on the bark. Then put a dab of glue under each piece and let them dry. Glue a loop of string on the back for a hanger.

Notes:

The best part of this is going on a nature walk to gather the materials. I give each child a basket to put his or her finds in.

We use a stronger glue than white school glue for this one, so I supervise the glueing process very carefully.

COLLAGE EXPERIENCE #2

OBJECTIVES

Tactile/Kinesthetic Awareness
Fine Motor — Writing Skills
Perceptual Motor — size

CHOICES

MEDIUM (S)	IMPLEMENT (S)	SURFACE (S)
Rope – all sizes	Strong glue	Denim — big enough to accomodate the amount of medium you have gathered
String		
Yarn		
Ribbon		

SUGGESTED DIRECTIONS

Arrange the medium in loops or in straight lines.
Make a picture.
Make a design.
Make your name.
Glue the medium to the denim.

Notes:

Making happy or sad faces and giving it lots of hair and those little plastic wobbly eyes is one of our favorites. I also like to use metallic yarn and string.

COLLAGE EXPERIENCE #3

OBJECTIVES

Tactile/Kinesthetic Awareness
Fine Motor
Concept Development — size, body parts

CHOICES

MEDIUM (S)	IMPLEMENT (S)	SURFACE (S)
Flat rocks of all sizes	Strong glue	Weathered board to accomodate the number of rocks you have.
Black marker– fine line	Thin rope or picture hanger	
	hammer	
	nails	

SUGGESTED DIRECTIONS

After you have gathered your rocks, make faces on all of them. Then glue them on the board. Glue the rope in a loop on the back so you can hang it up, or nail the picture hanger on the back.

Notes:

We called our composition The Flat Rock Family Reunion. We had an uncle rock that was sad because he hated reunions. We had a very happy aunt rock that loved the food. We had little children rocks and grandparent rocks.

Use a glue strong enough to hold the rocks on the wood and supervise its use carefully.

COLLAGE EXPERIENCE #4

OBJECTIVES

Tactile/Kinesthetic Awareness
Fine Motor
Perceptual Motor

CHOICES

MEDIUM (S)	IMPLEMENT (S)	SURFACE (S)
Stickers that require moistening	Sponge/water or tongue	Notebook paper so we can save our stickers

SUGGESTED DIRECTIONS

Hold the smallest surface of the sticker. Moisten it either with your tongue or with a sponge. I prefer the tongue because then you get to experience the taste of the glue.

Don't overlick it. It won't stick. Press it on the surface. Smooth it out if you need to.

Notes:

I like the stickers that you can use to create a scene or dress a sticker figure with.

COLLAGE EXPERIENCE #5

OBJECTIVES

Tactile/Kinesthetic Awareness
Fine Motor
Writing Skills
Concept Development — size

CHOICES

MEDIUM (S)	IMPLEMENT (S)	SURFACE (S)
Egg shells — at least six eggs	Plastic bag White school glue	Cardboard

SUGGESTED DIRECTIONS

Either boil the egg and remove the shell when it is cool or punch small holes in the ends of the shells and blow the egg out uncooked.

Put the egg shell in the bag.

Roll, punch, squeeze the bag until the egg shells are in the desired size pieces.

Put glue on the surface and carefully place the egg shell in place or sprinkle it onto the glue.

Make a picture, an egg shell tower, your name or a design. When it dries, run your fingers over it.

Notes:

This experience was the turning point for a tactile defensive child with autism. After wrinkling his nose, trying to avoid it, hiding his hands behind his back, quietly sneaking back to his space, etc., he gave it a try. He actually got quite a bit of egg shell on the cardboard before he could take no more. After this he tried everything else more quickly and with less and less distaste. I guess he figured I couldn't come up with anything more gross. (P.S. – I did.)

COLLAGE EXPERIENCE #6

OBJECTIVES

Tactile/Kinesthetic Awareness
Fine Motor
Writing Skills
Concept Development — colors

CHOICES

MEDIUM (S)	IMPLEMENT (S)	SURFACE (S)
Cottonballs — blue and white	White school glue	Construction paper

SUGGESTED DIRECTIONS

Dab glue on the surface.
Put a cottonball on the glue.
Make a picture or just make a design.
Make your name.

Notes:

For children who have trouble putting the glue on and sticking the cotton down, I have found it helpful to put the glue on the surface for the child and let the child stick the cotton on. This helps to build on the child's attention span and gives them directionality.

COLLAGE EXPERIENCE #7

OBJECTIVES

Fine Motor
Functional Living Skills

CHOICES

MEDIUM (S)	IMPLEMENT (S)	SURFACE (S)
Paper Plate	Strong glue	Piece of cardboard, size of a placemat. Can be covered in contact paper.
Paper Cup		
Paper Napkin		
Plastic fork, knife, & spoon		

SUGGESTED DIRECTIONS

Arrange item in proper placement on the placemat.
Glue down.
Refer to when setting the table.

Notes:

This arrangement looks interesting when you hang it on the wall.

I like to use a napkin from the child's favorite restaurant. If it has a good logo on it, the child will identify it proudly. This is a good reading activity.

COLLAGE EXPERIENCE #8

OBJECTIVES

Tactile/Kinesthetic Awareness
Fine Motor
Perceptual Motor
Concept Development — texture

CHOICES

MEDIUM (S)	IMPLEMENT (S)	SURFACE (S)
Aluminum foil	Strong glue	Pretty piece of wallpaper
Wax paper		
Plastic wrap		
Sandpaper		

SUGGESTED DIRECTIONS

Smash the different materials into balls. Glue on the surface.
Make a picture. Make your name. Make a design.
See how tall you can make it.

Notes:

One of my third grade students handed me a foil wrapped present for Christmas one year. I started to unwrap it, and he screwed his face up and looked miserable. "Oh, I'll wait until later", I said, thinking he was embarrassed for me to open it in front of everyone. "No, no", he said. "Do you want me to open it now?", I asked him. He started to cry. One of the other children whispered to me, "It is open."

For several years I used bits and pieces of this aluminum foil ball in art experiences. It lasted a long time.

COLLAGE EXPERIENCE #9

OBJECTIVES

Fine Motor
Tactile/Kinesthetic Awareness
Writing Skills
Concept Development — shapes

CHOICES

MEDIUM (S)	IMPLEMENT (S)	SURFACE (S)
Uncooked pasta — all shapes	White school glue	Foam dinner plates

SUGGESTED DIRECTIONS

Glue the pasta down in all possible combinations.
Pile it as high as you can.
Make your name. Make a face. Make a design.

Notes:

When we are finished with our creations, we usually splash a little red paint on them for sauce.
When they are dry we put them in our play kitchen to be used for imaginary meals.

COLLAGE EXPERIENCE #10

OBJECTIVES

Fine Motor
Tactile/Kinesthetic Awareness

CHOICES

MEDIUM (S)	IMPLEMENT (S)	SURFACE (S)
Newspaper	White school glue	Large piece of cardboard. 2' x 2' is a good size.

SUGGESTED DIRECTIONS

Get the newspaper from your paper tear (from Play Experience #4), or tear up fresh paper.
Glue it down flat.
Glue only a small piece of it so it hangs off the cardboard.
Twist it before you glue it down.
Try to make shapes that stand up.

Notes:

I like doing this as a group. We all build on each other's creation and it becomes a sharing activity.

You can also use colored tissue paper, paper towels, or wrapping paper for this activity. You can use them individually or mix them up.

(See Play Experience #4)

COLLAGE EXPERIENCE #11

OBJECTIVES

Tactile/Kinesthetic Awareness
Fine Motor
Writing Skills
Concept Development — size

CHOICES

MEDIUM (S)	IMPLEMENT (S)	SURFACE (S)
Popcorn	White school glue	Cardboard — painted or cover with construction paper
Beans		
Rice		

SUGGESTED DIRECTIONS

Glue the construction paper to the cardboard.
Make a design with the beans, rice and popcorn.
Make your name. Make a picture. Make a progression from small to big.

Notes:

Some children have to be reminded that it isn't lunch time and we don't eat the mediums.

COLLAGE EXPERIENCE #12

OBJECTIVES

Tactile/Kinesthetic Awareness
Fine Motor
Perceptual Motor
Concept Development — colors

CHOICES

MEDIUM (S)	IMPLEMENT (S)	SURFACE (S)
Feathers — all colors	Strong glue	Velvet

SUGGESTED DIRECTIONS

Place the feathers on the velvet and glue down.

Notes:

I outline a bird on velvet with chalk and let the children glue the feathers on the bird. You can buy brightly colored feathers from a craft store.

COLLAGE EXPERIENCE #13

OBJECTIVES

Tactile/Kinesthetic Awareness
Fine Motor
Perceptual Motor
Writing Skills

CHOICES

MEDIUM (S)	IMPLEMENT (S)	SURFACE (S)
Bolts	Strong glue	Piece of wood
Nuts		
Screws		
Big Nails		

SUGGESTED DIRECTIONS

Glue the bolts, screws, etc. on the wood.
Make a design. Make a picture. Make your name.

Notes:

We like to make bolt, nut, screw, nail people. When they are finished and all dry, they are great to run your fingers over and over.

COLLAGE EXPERIENCE #14

OBJECTIVES

Tactile/Kinesthetic Awareness
Fine Motor
Perceptual Motor

CHOICES

MEDIUM (S)	IMPLEMENT (S)	SURFACE (S)
Cloth — velvet, felt, burlap, knit, fake fur, lace, vinyl, corduroy, terry cloth, leather, denim, gauze, etc.	Strong glue	Cardboard

SUGGESTED DIRECTIONS

Cut the fabric in interesting shapes.
Glue the cloth down at random or make a design.

Notes:

I cut the cardboard into the shape of a piece of clothing before we start glueing. When you are finished, it looks similar to a rag coat.

COLLAGE EXPERIENCE #15

OBJECTIVES

Perceptual Motor
Tactile/Kinesthetic Awareness
Fine Motor
Concept Development — colors, size, texture

CHOICES

MEDIUM (S)	IMPLEMENT (S)	SURFACE (S)
Buttons — all colors, all sizes	Strong glue	Ribbon — at least 2" wide

SUGGESTED DIRECTIONS

Glue the buttons on the ribbon, going down.
Go from biggest button to smallest.
Go from prettiest to ugliest.
Go from brightest to dullest.

Notes:

I have everybody bring in 10 buttons if they can spare them. We mix them all up and use them for this experience as well as for sewing, and occasionally we use one when someone loses a button off their clothes.

COLLAGE EXPERIENCE #16

OBJECTIVES

Perceptual Motor
Tactile/Kinesthetic Awareness
Fine Motor
Concept Development — colors, sizes, shapes, texture

CHOICES

MEDIUM (S)	IMPLEMENT (S)	SURFACE (S)
Sponges — all colors	White school glue	Burlap – natural
Corks — all sizes		

SUGGESTED DIRECTIONS

Cut the sponges into shapes.
Glue down on the burlap. Add the corks.
Make a design. Make a picture. Make your name.

Notes:

I like the combination of sponges and burlap.
Also, sponges give when you push on them. The corks, even though they look similar, do not give. An interesting contrast.

COLLAGE EXPERIENCE #17

OBJECTIVES

Tactile/Kinesthetic Awareness
Fine Motor
Concept Development — size, texture

CHOICES

MEDIUM (S)	IMPLEMENT (S)	SURFACE (S)
Cotton balls	Paint rolling tray	Cardboard tubes —
Rice	White school glue	paper towels, wrapping paper, toilet tissue, etc.

SUGGESTED DIRECTIONS

Put a thin layer of glue in the tray.
Roll the tube in the glue. Make sure it is all covered with glue.
Lay the cotton balls on a table and roll the tube over the cotton balls. Let dry.
Roll the cotton ball covered tube through the glue.
Spread rice out. Roll through the rice.

Notes:

I run a string through the top of these and hang them from the ceiling. You can then attach another tube to the bottom of the first or hang them individually.

PAINTING EXPERIENCES
47 Experiences

Author's Note:

I add liquid hand soap to most painting experiences because it makes for easier clean-up!
I use hand soap because it is gentler than dish soap.

CHOICES FOR PAINTING EXPERIENCES

MEDIUM	IMPLEMENT	SURFACE
Paint —	string	gourds
acrylic house paint	bowl	paper —
water colors	hands	construction
poster paint	cotton swabs	finger paint
finger paint	vegetable brush	paper plate
food coloring	paper cups	cardboard —
water	rolls —	smooth
liquid hand soap	paper towel	corrugated
vaseline	toilet tissue	wrapping
sand	wrapping paper	wax
cornmeal	carpet	newspaper
beans	mittens	wallpaper
rice	balloons	bags
glitter	comb	sand
egg shells	hair brush	window shade
pasta	fruits	aluminum foil
glue	vegetables	floor
bar soap	markers	
soap bubbles	pine cone	
plastic fork	rubber gloves	
plastic knife	bubble wand	
plastic spoon	dog	
construction paper	paint tray	
	flowers	
	sponges —	
	dish	
	car	
	mop	

PAINTING EXPERIENCE #1

OBJECTIVES

Fine Motor
Perceptual Motor
Writing Skills
Concept Development — colors

CHOICES

MEDIUM (S)	IMPLEMENT (S)	SURFACE (S)
Water colors — basic colors	Cotton swabs	White construction paper
Water		

SUGGESTED DIRECTIONS

Dip the cotton swab in water and dab it on the paper.
Drag it on the paper.
Write with it.
Draw with it.

Notes:

This experience makes me think of chinese drawings and paintings.
The cotton swab makes such a delicate mark on the paper.
You can make some wonderful pastel colored, dreamy pictures.

PAINTING EXPERIENCE #2

OBJECTIVES

Tactile/Kinesthetic Awareness
Fine Motor
Perceptual Motor
Concept Development — colors

CHOICES

MEDIUM (S)	IMPLEMENT (S)	SURFACE (S)
Poster paint — black	Balloons	White construction paper
Liquid hand soap		

SUGGESTED DIRECTIONS

Mix the paint with a little soap.

Blow the balloons up.
Don't make them so big that you can't grab hold of them easily and manipulate them.
Tie the ends.

Dip the balloon in the paint and blot it on the paper.
Rub it on the paper.
Drag it on the paper.

Notes:

We play with the balloons first as in the play experience section, (See Play Experience #9).
We go into a room and bat the balloons around. Afterwards, the child is ready to explore something else to do with the balloon besides throw it and bop it.

PAINTING EXPERIENCE #3

OBJECTIVES

Tactile/Kinesthetic Awareness
Fine Motor
Perceptual Motor
Concept Development — colors

CHOICES

MEDIUM (S)	IMPLEMENT (S)	SURFACE (S)
Poster paint — white	Strawberry carton —	Terry cloth
Liquid hand soap	plastic with open weave design	

SUGGESTED DIRECTIONS

Mix the paint with a little soap.
Place a thin layer on a paper plate.
Press the carton into the paint.
Press the carton on to the terry cloth.
Keep the images separate or overlap them.

Notes:

Another way to do this is to place the carton on the surface and dip a brush in the paint and paint the bottom of the carton. Then lift it up.

PAINTING EXPERIENCE #4

OBJECTIVES

Gross Motor
Concept Development — colors, size

CHOICES

MEDIUM (S)	IMPLEMENT (S)	SURFACE (S)
Acrylic house paint — white	Paint roller with handle Paint tray	Large cardboard box (appliance box)

SUGGESTED DIRECTIONS

Pour the paint into the tray. Practice rolling the roller in the paint and taking off some of the paint before putting on the surface. You can drag the roller to the high part of the tray and roll some paint out or drag the roller across the edge of the tray. Maybe you have other tricks.
Roll the paint onto the cardboard box.

Notes:

We turned our freshly painted box into a house. I took different colored plastic film (the stuff you get at Easter time) and made a red, blue and yellow window. My students with autism love to look through these colored windows. I still like to view the world through rose colored glasses, myself. Next time someone is involved in a house painting project and the child indicates that they can help, they probably will be able to because they've had practice!

PAINTING EXPERIENCE #5

OBJECTIVES

Tactile/Kinesthetic Awareness
Concept Development — colors, textures

CHOICES

MEDIUM (S)	IMPLEMENT (S)	SURFACE (S)
Poster paint — purple, red and yellow	Shag carpet — cut into strips around 2" x 4"	Burlap

SUGGESTED DIRECTIONS

Mix the paint with a little soap.
Dip the carpet strip in the paint mixture.
Use just the tip of the carpet strip, or bend it over and use a large portion of the end.
Drag it across the burlap.
We tape the burlap down so it does not move all over the place while we are creating.
Blot the carpet strip on the burlap.
Use the back of the carpet strip to apply the paint.

Notes:

Our finished piece resembled a floral design. I kept it hanging in the classroom the entire year.

It was created by an integrated group of first and second grade children with autism, and third and fourth grade children without autism.

PAINTING EXPERIENCE #6

OBJECTIVES

Fine Motor
Writing Skills
Perceptual Motor
Concept Development — colors, sizes

CHOICES

MEDIUM (S)	IMPLEMENT (S)	SURFACE (S)
Poster paint — red, yellow	Cooking baster	Vinyl
Liquid hand soap	Eye dropper	

SUGGESTED DIRECTIONS

Mix the paint with a little soap.
Fill the cooking baster with the red paint and dribble or gush it all over the vinyl.
Fill the eye dropper with yellow paint and dribble or gush it all over the vinyl.
Compare the two. Did the baster make a different pattern than the eye dropper?
What color did the two paints make when they met each other on the vinyl.

Notes:

This is another good tool to make the child's name with. That personalization of the experience is important to children.

PAINTING EXPERIENCE #7

OBJECTIVES

Tactile/Kinesthetic Awareness
Perceptual Motor
Fine Motor
Concept Development — colors, body parts

CHOICES

MEDIUM (S)	IMPLEMENT (S)	SURFACE (S)
Water colors — basic colors	Soft paint brush	Face
		Mirror

SUGGESTED DIRECTIONS

Mix the paint with a little soap.
Dip brush in water color and paint child's face while they watch in the mirror.
Let the child paint your face.
Let the child clean his/her face and paint their own face.
Let the child paint another child's face.
Let the child paint his/her face on the mirror.
Discuss body parts while painting them.

Notes:

I like to use an instant camera and photograph the child's face before and after painting. The child can watch their picture develop, and we can use the picture for language lessons, body awareness, or creative writing.

Always find out if the child has allergic reactions before you start painting them.
Hives are not a pretty picture and could really turn a child and their parents or guardians off to your art program.

PAINTING EXPERIENCE #8

OBJECTIVES

Perceptual Motor
Gross Motor
Concept Development — colors, directionality

CHOICES

MEDIUM (S)	IMPLEMENT (S)	SURFACE (S)
Poster paint — green	Small broom	Wrapping paper
Liquid hand soap	Large broom	or largest piece of paper you can find
	Push broom	

SUGGESTED DIRECTIONS

Mix the paint with a little soap.
Start with the small broom. Sweep the broom through the paint, then sweep it on the paper.
Repeat with the large broom which will probably be harder to control.
Use the push broom.

Notes:

It is probably a good idea to do this activity outside. If you can't do it outside, put down a large piece of plastic. (Painter's drop cloth, old shower curtain, etc.)

PAINTING EXPERIENCE #9

OBJECTIVES

Fine Motor
Perceptual Motor
Writing Skills
Concept Development — colors, texture

CHOICES

MEDIUM (S)	IMPLEMENT (S)	SURFACE (S)
Finger nail polish —	Finger nail polish brush	Black construction paper
Bottle of red	Sprinkle sparkle jar	
Bottle of clear		
Sparkles		

SUGGESTED DIRECTIONS

Make design, picture, name, etc. with clear nail polish.
Trace with red nail polish.
Sprinkle with sparkles before the polish dries.

Notes:

Opening the small bottle can be a challenge for a child.
There is something about the little fingernail polish bottle with its own little brush that intrigued my students with autism.

One little girl beamed when she saw the bottle and kept sticking her hands out to me. When we finished our names, I painted her nails. She is a very active young lady, and this was the longest she had set still.

PAINTING EXPERIENCE #10

OBJECTIVES

Gross Motor
Concept Development — colors

CHOICES

MEDIUM (S)	IMPLEMENT (S)	SURFACE (S)
Finger paint — yellow	Potato masher —	Red construction paper
Liquid hand soap	with the holes in the end	

SUGGESTED DIRECTIONS

Mix the paint with a little soap.
Hold the handle of the masher and place it in the paint.
Place it on the paper. Pick it up and put it down.
Rub it on the paper.
Drag it on the paper.

Notes:

I use finger paint for this experience because it is thicker and clings to the potato masher.
We did this on grass one time. The grass was mowed before it rained, and it was interesting to
see how our designs changed after the grass was cut.

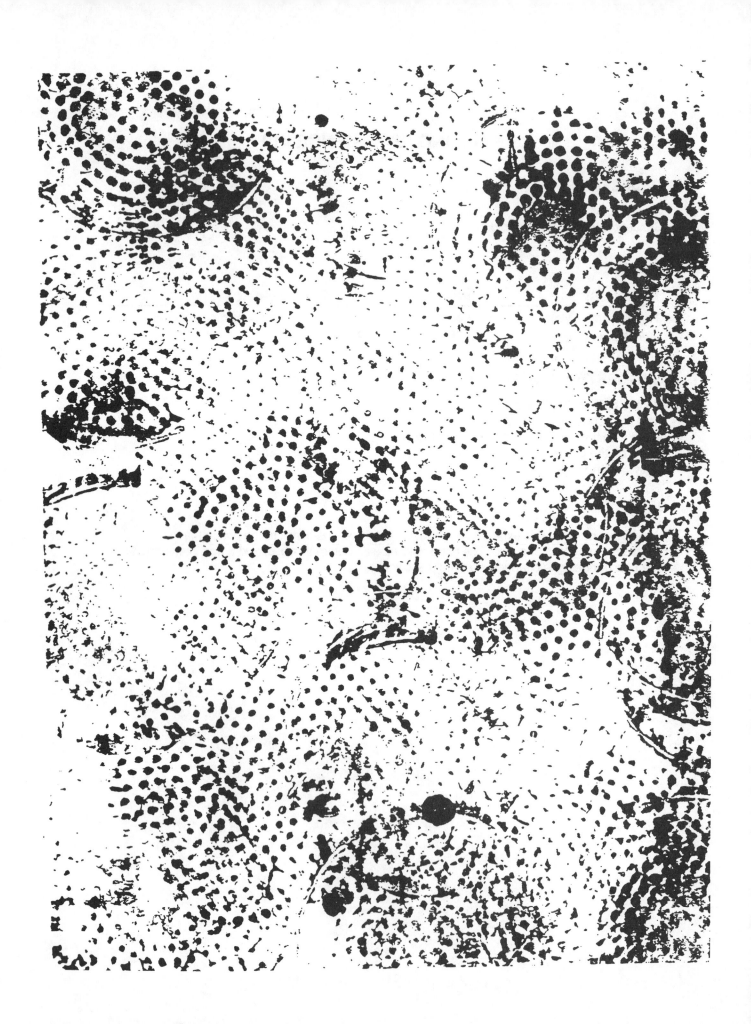

PAINTING EXPERIENCE #11

OBJECTIVES

Tactile/Kinesthetic Awareness
Perceptual Motor
Fine Motor
Concept Development — colors, temperature

CHOICES

MEDIUM (S)	IMPLEMENT (S)	SURFACE (S)
Ice cubes	Hands	White finger paint paper
Finger paints — blue		
Liquid hand soap		

SUGGESTED DIRECTIONS

Put an egg sized gob of blue paint on the paper. Plop the ice cube into the paint. Add a little soap. Move the ice cube through the paint and all over the paper.

Try to keep going until the ice cube is melted.

Notes:

We used blue paint because it reminded us of the ocean.
Two second grade children raced to see who's ice cube would melt first. (A good science lesson.)
A first grade child with minimal vision and hearing was at first a little startled that the usual paint was so cold. . . Then became delighted with the whole experience and went through three ice cubes.
A third grade child with autism attempted to suck on the ice cube. Well, it was a pretty hot day. We took a break and had frozen treats.

PAINTING EXPERIENCE #12

OBJECTIVES

Fine Motor
Perceptual Motor
Concept Development — colors

CHOICES

MEDIUM (S)	IMPLEMENT (S)	SURFACE (S)
Finger paint — blue	Food grater (flat type)	Paper plate
Liquid hand soap	Scrub pad	
	Bowl a little smaller than grater	

SUGGESTED DIRECTIONS

Put the paper plate in the bottom of the bowl.
Put the grater on top of the bowl.
Mix the paint with a little soap.
Put a glob of paint on top of the grater.
Use the scrub pad to swish the paint back and forth across the grater until most of the paint goes through onto the surface.

Notes:

The end result depends on the intensity with which the child scrubs on the grater. It can be a splatter effect or just a dribble effect.

PAINTING EXPERIENCE #13

OBJECTIVES

Tactile/Kinesthetic Awareness
Gross Motor
Concept Development — colors

CHOICES

MEDIUM (S)	IMPLEMENT (S)	SURFACE (S)
Poster paint — red, yellow, and blue	Old shoes — tennis, football, high heels, etc.	Large piece of cardboard
	Socks	
	Bare feet	

SUGGESTED DIRECTIONS

Mix the paint with a little soap.
Let the child select a pair of shoes and a color.
Put the shoes on and walk through the color and on to the cardboard.
Hop, skip, dance, jump, slide, etc.

Do three children per piece of cardboard with each child using a different color paint.

The same three children repeat the experience with old socks, using the same color paint on a new cardboard.

The same three children repeat the experience with bare feet, using the same color paint on a new cardboard.

Notes:

This experience can be a little slippery when using bare feet, so have helping hands ready to support the one in the paint.

We have done this on the sidewalk, and it is fun to watch the feet disappear with rain and time.

PAINTING EXPERIENCE #14

OBJECTIVES

Fine Motor
Perceptual Motor
Concept Development — colors, shapes

CHOICES

MEDIUM (S)	IMPLEMENT (S)	SURFACE (S)
Poster paint — red, yellow, and blue	Spray bottle (for plants, cleaning liquid, etc.)	Sidewalk
Liquid hand soap		Cardboard cut into shapes (circle, square, triangle)
Water		

SUGGESTED DIRECTIONS

Fill the spray bottle with paint and a little soap.
Place a shape on the sidewalk.
Stand above it and spray until it is covered.
Remove the cardboard and look at the shape you made.
Wait until it rains or snows and see what happened to your shape.

Notes:

We always experiment with the type spray we want. A lot of bottles have a stream or a spray to choose from.

PAINTING EXPERIENCE #15

OBJECTIVES

Perceptual Motor
Gross Motor
Fine Motor
Concept Development — colors, temperature

CHOICES

MEDIUM (S)	IMPLEMENT (S)	SURFACE (S)
Snow	Hands	Snow
Water Colors — basic colors	Paint brushes	

SUGGESTED DIRECTIONS

Make a snow object.
Pack it tight.
Paint your object with the water colors.

Notes:

I had a creative teacher in elementary school. Her eyes sparkled as she led us on many free spirited adventures. One was making a huge snow creature during a softly falling snow. When we were finished, she produced water paints and brushes and we painted our creature.
It was the most beautiful sight. How I cried when it finally melted. I think of this experience every winter and have repeated it with many of my own students.

If you live in a warmer climate —
make snow using ice cubes and a blender, or use a sno-cone machine.

PAINTING EXPERIENCE #16

OBJECTIVES

Perceptual Motor
Fine Motor
Speech and language
Concept Development — colors, shapes

CHOICES

MEDIUM (S)	IMPLEMENT (S)	SURFACE (S)
Soap bubbles	Bubble wand	White finger paint paper
Food coloring — red		

SUGGESTED DIRECTIONS

Add a few drops of the food coloring to the bubbles.
Dip the wand in and blow onto the paper.
If you want a more intense color, add more coloring.

Notes:

Don't stand too close to the paper or the bubbles will splatter in your face and give you freckles.
We like to put the paper on the floor and stand over it. If the bubble liquid drips, it then drips onto the picture and becomes part of it.
This is a good activity for children who are having delays in speech.
The act of blowing is an important part of speech development.

PAINTING EXPERIENCE #17

OBJECTIVES

Fine Motor
Perceptual Motor
Writing Skills
Concept Development — colors, size

CHOICES

MEDIUM (S)	IMPLEMENT (S)	SURFACE (S)
Poster paint — yellow	Large funnel	Sandpaper — medium
Liquid hand soap	Small funnel	

SUGGESTED DIRECTIONS

Mix the paint with a little soap.
One person holds the funnel over the paper while another person pours the paint into the funnel.
The paint should be of the right consistency to flow through the funnel.
You can move the funnel around to create a line or let the paint drip out for a dot effect.
Make your name.
Make a design.

Notes:

When we have too much paint on our surface, we sometimes pick the sandpaper up, tilting it different ways, to create an entirely new design. The children like to watch the paint flow this way and that.

PAINTING EXPERIENCE #18

OBJECTIVES

Fine Motor
Gross Motor
Perceptual Motor
Concept Development — colors, directionality

CHOICES

MEDIUM (S)	IMPLEMENT (S)	SURFACE (S)
Poster paint — brown	Battery operated tank	Brown wrapping paper (Large piece)
Liquid hand soap		

SUGGESTED DIRECTIONS

Mix the paint with a little soap.
Turn the toy on and place it on the paper.
When it comes close to the edge, grab it and turn it around.

Notes:

When my son's toys disappear for a few days then reappear with traces of paint on them, he knows I've used them for an art experience. He doesn't get upset anymore, he just wants to repeat the fun at home.
I like the tank because of the treads. We chose brown paint because it looked like mud.
This experience allows children without good fine motor control, the ability to at least turn the item on and watch as someone else controls it. A first grade boy with cerebral palsy was able to turn the tank on with much hard work and concentration and giggled and giggled when it ran around on the paper. He worked very hard at getting it turned off, too, and therefore become an active participant in this experience. You can also try a wind up toy or a remote control toy for this experience.

PAINTING EXPERIENCE #19

OBJECTIVES

Tactile/Kinesthetic Awareness
Fine Motor
Perceptual Motor
Concept Development — colors

CHOICES

MEDIUM (S)	IMPLEMENT (S)	SURFACE (S)
Poster paint — purple	Fat pine cone	White construction paper
Liquid hand soap		

SUGGESTED DIRECTIONS

Mix the paint with a little soap.
Roll the pine cone in the paint.
Roll, tap, drag, drop, etc. onto the paper.

Notes:

Save the purple pine cone to make a nature collage.
(See Collage Experience #1, pp. 11)

PAINTING EXPERIENCE #20

OBJECTIVES

Fine Motor
Gross Motor
Writing Skills
Concept Development — colors, size

CHOICES

MEDIUM (S)	IMPLEMENT (S)	SURFACE (S)
Poster paint — red, yellow, blue	Big pitcher	Pressed board 24" x 24"
Liquid hand soap	Small pitcher (Different types of spouts)	

SUGGESTED DIRECTIONS

Mix the paint with a little soap.
Choose a color and a pitcher. Put about an inch of paint in the pitcher. Hold over the surface and pour. Make a design, make your name, make a picture, etc.

Notes:

Save this work of art to do a collage on. This experience may cause splashing so make sure the children are well covered. . . and of course make sure you are covered, also.

PAINTING EXPERIENCE #21

OBJECTIVES

Gross Motor (for the horse)
Fine Motor
Speech and Language
Perceptual Motor
Concept Development — colors, directionality

CHOICES

MEDIUM (S)	IMPLEMENT (S)	SURFACE (S)
Poster paint — green Liquid hand soap	Plastic horse — any size easily held	Cardboard

SUGGESTED DIRECTIONS

Mix the paint with a little soap.
Hold the horse so you can get his feet in the paint and "dunt dun a lun dunt a lun lun lun" him through the paint.
Then, "dunt dun a lun dunt a lun lun lun" him on the cardboard.
The horse can walk, trot, gallop, even rear up. Occasionally we have had horses fall down.

Notes:

The gallopping sound effects are very contagious. Non-verbal children will be captivated by this sound and try to imitate it.

Not a good activity to be demonstrating if a left brained administrator walks into the room!

PAINTING EXPERIENCE #22

OBJECTIVES

Visual Awareness
Fine Motor
Perceptual Motor

CHOICES

MEDIUM (S)	IMPLEMENT (S)	SURFACE (S)
Darkness	Fat paint brushes	Large sheets of white construction paper
Poster paint — black	Blindfold	
Liquid hand soap		

SUGGESTED DIRECTIONS

Mix the paint with a little soap.
Turn out the lights. Pull down the shades.
Put on a blindfold and paint.
Try to make picture.
Just make a design.
Take off the blindfold and look at what you did.

Notes:

You can talk about how people who are blind depend on other senses than their eyes.

PAINTING EXPERIENCE #23

OBJECTIVES

Fine Motor
Perceptual Motor
Speech and Language
Concept Development — colors, directionality

CHOICES

MEDIUM (S)	IMPLEMENT (S)	SURFACE (S)
Poster paint — black	Cars — little, big, with fat wheels, with skinny wheels	Paper bag
Liquid hand soap		

SUGGESTED DIRECTIONS

Mix the paint with a little soap.
Drive the car through the paint. Drive the car on the paper.

Have one child drive on the paper. Let another child match the car and try to stay on the first child's road using another color.

Have one child at one end of the paper and another child at the other end and drive the car through the paint then push it to each other.

Notes:

It is a very hard thing to do this activity without going vrooooom.
Several of my non-verbal children began imitating this sound.

PAINTING EXPERIENCE #24

OBJECTIVES

Tactile/Kinesthetic Awareness
Fine Motor
Perceptual Motor
Concept Development — colors, size, shapes

CHOICES

MEDIUM (S)	IMPLEMENT (S)	SURFACE (S)
Poster paint — red, yellow, blue, green	Golf ball, Tennis ball, Nerf ball, Small football, basketball	Felt
Liquid hand soap		

SUGGESTED DIRECTIONS

Mix the paint with a little soap.
Roll the golf ball in the red paint. Roll it on the felt.
Roll the tennis ball on the yellow paint. Roll it on the felt.
Roll the nerf ball in the blue paint. Roll it on the felt.
Roll the small football in the green paint. Roll it on the felt.

Two children can stand across a table from each other with felt on the table and roll the ball back and forth to each other.

Notes:

We especially like the design the golf ball makes. When we have free time with access to art, many of the children will choose to do ball painting.
I like to integrate handicapped and non-handicapped children for the joint painting effort. It encourages sharing and also provides models for appropriate social behavior that handicapped children so often need.

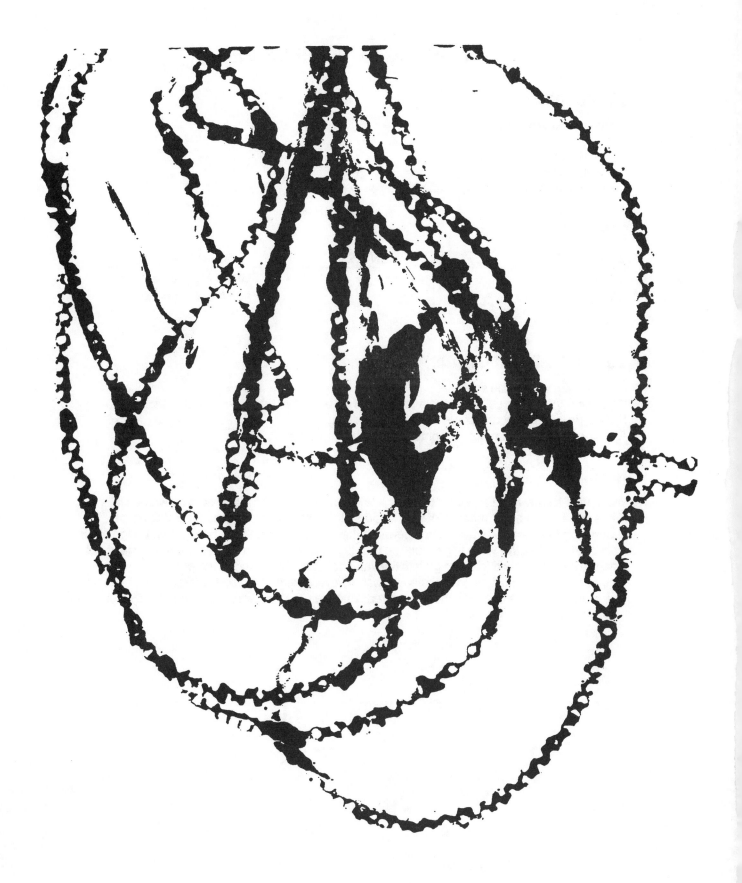

PAINTING EXPERIENCE #25

OBJECTIVES

Tactile/Kinesthetic Awareness
Fine Motor
Gross Motor
Perceptual Motor
Concept Development — colors, directionality

CHOICES

MEDIUM (S)	IMPLEMENT (S)	SURFACE (S)
Finger paint — glow in the dark	Hands	White finger paint paper taped to the ceiling
Liquid hand soap		

SUGGESTED DIRECTIONS

Mix the paint with a little soap.
Tape the paper to the ceiling. Have a child stand on a chair or table to reach the paper.
Put hands in the paint and press them on the ceiling.
After the hands dry, turn out the lights and watch them glow.

Notes:

We have a supply room at school that has a lower ceiling than the classroom so we use it.
Years ago I had a bright purple VW van. It had stained glass windows, multi-colored carpet
squares on the floor and walls, beads between the driver's seat and the back. I had bought it fur-
nished and cheap. We were finger painting with flourescent paints and I led the entire class out
onto the parking lot and let them go into the van and press their hand to the ceiling, then sign
their name. When I sold the van, the buyer was so overwhelmed by the general gaudiness that
they didn't notice the ceiling. I often wondered what their reaction was when they finally looked up!

PAINTING EXPERIENCE #26

OBJECTIVES

Fine Motor
Perceptual Motor
Concept Development — colors

CHOICES

MEDIUM (S)	IMPLEMENT (S)	SURFACE (S)
Permanent Markers— red, yellow, blue, green, black, purple, brown	The marker case	Cotton squares (12" x 12")

SUGGESTED DIRECTIONS

Tape the cloth to a table top. We used the theme "Happy Blocks", with the child making a picture of whatever made them happy. (See "Arts and Activities", January, 1975, page 21)
Put newspaper under the square before you tape it down. The ink will go through the cotton.

Notes:

I sewed all of the squares together and made a quilt.
Another time I used larger pieces of material and made throw pillows for my living room.
A plain pillow slip can be decorated and makes a nice remembrance of a special group or an excellent gift for the child to give.

PAINTING EXPERIENCE #27

OBJECTIVES

Fine Motor
Perceptual Motor
Writing Skills
Concept Development — colors

CHOICES

MEDIUM (S)	IMPLEMENT (S)	SURFACE (S)
Poster paint — red	Small paddle	Denim (12" x 12")
Liquid hand soap	(without the ball attached)	

SUGGESTED DIRECTIONS

Mix the paint with a little soap.
Put the paddle in the paint.
Drag, tap, draw, write with the paddle on the denim.

Notes:

I like the look of the red paint on the denim.
These can have the edges frayed and glued down on slats to make a nice wall hanging.

Also, if you are feeling adventurous —
Try using the paddle with the little ball attached. Bounce the ball in the paint, and then onto the surface. It makes a wonderful mess!

PAINTING EXPERIENCE #28

OBJECTIVES

Fine Motor
Perceptual Motor
Concept Development — colors, shapes, texture

CHOICES

MEDIUM (S)	IMPLEMENT (S)	SURFACE (S)
Poster paint — red, yellow, blue	Paint brush	Rocks — smooth, rough, big, little
Liquid hand soap		

SUGGESTED DIRECTIONS

Mix the paint with a little soap.
Go on a nature walk and gather rocks. Bring back whatever you can carry.
Paint faces, pictures, designs, etc. on the rocks.

Notes:

If you have a child, I am sure that at one time or another you have received a painted rock to be used as a paper weight. I have one on my bookshelf that is a treasured item. It is painted gold with the date added by the teacher.
Another variation of this experience is to use the rock as a paint brush and control the paint on the surface with it.

PAINTING EXPERIENCE #29

OBJECTIVES

Fine Motor
Perceptual Motor
Writing Skills
Concept Development — colors

CHOICES

MEDIUM (S)	IMPLEMENT (S)	SURFACE (S)
Poster paint — red	Dish mops —	Wax paper
Liquid hand soap	Sponge or string	

SUGGESTED DIRECTIONS

Mix the paint with a little soap.
Dip, drag, swirl the mop in the paint and dot, drag, swirl it on the paper.
Make a design.
Make a picture.
Make your name.

Notes:

All kinds of designs are possible with the mop, but the one design that almost every child can do is to tap it on the surface. This looks like a sponge octopus has walked across the surface. A second grade child with cerebral palsy was able to make a lovely creation with the mop. He plopped himself and me in the face a few times with the mop in the process, but the end result was something he was very proud of.
I like to use wax paper occasionally because of the reaction of the wax paper to the paint and of the paint to the wax paper.

PAINTING EXPERIENCE #30

OBJECTIVES

Tactile/Kinesthetic Awareness
Fine Motor
Gross Motor
Perceptual Motor
Writing Skills
Concept Development — colors, directionality

CHOICES

MEDIUM (S)	IMPLEMENT (S)	SURFACE (S)
Poster paint — blue	Sponges — all sizes	Wrapping paper
Liquid hand soap	dish sponge, car sponge	
	sponge mop	

SUGGESTED DIRECTIONS

Mix the paint with a little soap.
Dip the smaller sponges in the paint and dab on the surface.
Wipe on the surface.
Make a design.
Make a picture.
Make your name.
Use the sponge mop and try to duplicate what you did with the smaller sponges.

Notes:

Some of the children with multiple handicaps, and especially those in wheel chairs had the best time painting with the mop. They needed varying degrees of assistance, but they really got into it.

PAINTING EXPERIENCE #31

OBJECTIVES

Tactile/Kinesthetic Awareness
Gross Motor
Concept Development — colors, directionality

CHOICES

MEDIUM (S)	IMPLEMENT (S)	SURFACE (S)
Finger paint — red	Mittens	Newspaper
Liquid hand soap		

SUGGESTED DIRECTIONS

Hang the paper on the wall so the children can use their hands outstretched.
Mix the paint with a little soap.
Put the mittens on and put them in the paint.
Put the mittens on the paper.

Notes:

Some children do not like to wear mittens. For a fourth grade girl with autism who did not want to put the mittens on, we did the following: We let her hold the mittens and put them in the paint and on the paper. Next, she allowed us to tie the mitten to the palm of her hand, and finally she reluctantly put the mitten on, then became very agressive with the paint and the paper. She looked happy and her picture was great!
If she absolutely did not want to have anything to to with the mitten, what would I have done? Simply moved on to a new experience. However, I would have come back to this one another day.

PAINTING EXPERIENCE #32

OBJECTIVES

Tactile/Kinesthetic Awareness
Gross Motor
Perceptual Motor
Concept Development — colors

CHOICES

MEDIUM (S)	IMPLEMENT (S)	SURFACE (S)
Vaseline	Roll —	Aluminum foil
Finger paint — yellow	paper towel, wrapping paper, toilet tissue, etc.	
Liquid hand soap		

SUGGESTED DIRECTIONS

Mix the paint with a little soap.
Add a gob on vaseline and mix together.
Roll the roll in the mixture and roll it onto the aluminum foil.

Notes:

Since the vaseline does not dry, the finished product cannot be easily taken home. We usually admire it for a few days and check it out with our fingers and eventually we throw it away.

OR—
Transfer the paint to another surface so it becomes a whole new painting experience.

PAINTING EXPERIENCE #33

OBJECTIVES

Tactile/Kinesthetic Awareness
Fine Motor
Perceptual Motor
Concept Development — colors, size, shapes

CHOICES

MEDIUM (S)	IMPLEMENT (S)	SURFACE (S)
Poster paint — red, yellow, blue	Paper cups — at least three sizes	Velvet
Liquid hand soap		

SUGGESTED DIRECTIONS

Mix the paint with a little soap.
Spread a thin layer of paint on a paper plate.
Firmly press the rim of the cup into the paint.
Press the rim on the velvet.
Try all sizes.
Turn the cup over and use the bottom instead of the rim.
Go from smallest to biggest. Go from biggest to smallest.
Put the cups inside each other from biggest to smallest.

Notes:

We turn our circles into faces. We give them ears, noses, mouths, hair, etc.
You can use spools of all different sizes to make a similar effect.

PAINTING EXPERIENCE #34

OBJECTIVES

Tactile/Kinesthetic Awareness
Fine Motor
Perceptual Motor
Concept Development — colors, shapes, directionality

CHOICES

MEDIUM (S)	IMPLEMENT (S)	SURFACE (S)
Poster paint — black	Vegetable brush	Window shade
Liquid hand soap		

SUGGESTED DIRECTIONS

Mix the paint with a little soap.
Dip the vegetable brush in the paint.
Unwind the shade.
Press the brush onto the surface.

Notes:

We were getting new shades in a week or two so we decorated the old ones in the meantime.
The students in my behaviorally disturbed class seemed to like the idea that they had created
part of the decor, and perhaps a touch of acceptable graffiti! It gave them a sense of ownership
and belonging.

PAINTING EXPERIENCE #35

OBJECTIVES

Fine Motor
Perceptual Motor
Concept Development — colors, directionality

CHOICES

MEDIUM (S)	IMPLEMENT (S)	SURFACE (S)
Acrylic house paint — green, brown, orange	String Bowls or small buckets	Gourds — all sizes

SUGGESTED DIRECTIONS

Tie the string on the gourd.
Put enough paint in the bowl or bucket to cover the gourd.
Take a good look at the gourd.
What color is it?
Dip it in the container.
What color is it now?

Notes:

A lot of children will want to dip the gourd in more than one color. I encourage this inquisitiveness.

71

PAINTING EXPERIENCE #36

OBJECTIVES

Perceptual Motor
Fine Motor
Concept Development — colors, directionality

CHOICES

MEDIUM (S)	IMPLEMENT (S)	SURFACE (S)
Finer paint — red, yellow, blue	Large pic comb	white construction paper
	Large hair brush	
Liquid hand soap		

SUGGESTED DIRECTIONS

Put about a teaspoon full of red, yellow, blue paint at the top of the paper but no wider than the comb. Let the child pull the comb through the paint and down the paper until the paint gives out. Repeat the experience using the hair brush.

Notes:

I use the pic comb because of the handle. An option is to use many different sizes of combs.
We use these papers for greeting cards and wrapping paper.
The paper can be used for poster backgrounds, also.
Be alert for those who want to practice their self help skills. I have had children go home with multi-colored hair.

PAINTING EXPERIENCE #37

OBJECTIVES

Tactile/Kinesthetic Awareness
Fine Motor
Perceptual Motor
Concept Development — colors, shapes

CHOICES

MEDIUM (S)	IMPLEMENT (S)	SURFACE (S)
Poster paint — red, orange, green	Apple	White construction paper
	Orange	
Liquid hand soap	Cucumber	
	Black fine line marker	

SUGGESTED DIRECTIONS

Mix the paints with a little soap.
Slice the apple, orange and cucumber in halves.
Dip the apple in the paint and on the paper as many times as you wish.
Do the same with the orange and the cucumber.
Do all three on one paper or make a separate paper for each.
Use red for the apple, orange for the orange, and green for the cucumber, or mix the colors up and make the apple orange or green etc.
When dry, outline the shapes with the marker.

Notes:

We have cut our shapes out and made mobiles from them.
Also, the cucumber is especially fun to turn into people. I cut them lengthwise because it makes such an interesting shape, but they can also be cut in half and it makes a nice big handle to hold onto.
Make sure the children don't decide to take a bite when the objects are covered with paint.

PAINTING EXPERIENCE #38

OBJECTIVES

Tactile/Kinesthetic Awareness
Fine Motor
Writing Skills
Perceptual Motor
Concept Development — colors, texture

CHOICES

MEDIUM (S)	IMPLEMENT (S)	SURFACE (S)
Finger paint — brown	Hands	White finger paint paper
Sand or cornmeal		
Liquid hand soap		

SUGGESTED DIRECTIONS

Sand and cornmeal are very similar in the feel and the effect. I use whichever is handy.
Mix the sand or cornmeal or both into some fingerpaint and soap.
Swirl the mixture around on the surface.
Make a design.
Make a picture.
Make your name.

Notes:

We always make our names as one of our experiences. It is especially good for beginning readers to have the dry name to trace over and over.

PAINTING EXPERIENCE #39

OBJECTIVES

Tactile/Kinesthetic Awareness
Perceptual Motor
Fine Motor
Concept Development — colors, size

CHOICES

MEDIUM (S)	IMPLEMENT (S)	SURFACE (S)
Dry white beans/dry rice	Hands	Corrugated cardboard
Finger paint — red		
White school glue		

SUGGESTED DIRECTIONS

Mix some beans and rice with red finger paint and some white school glue.
Scoop the mixture onto the cardboard and swirl around. The rice will go into the grooves of the cardboard and the beans will stay on top.

Notes:

When the rice goes into the grooves and the beans stay on top this is a good time to talk about big and little.
You can take a bean and a piece of rice and glue them on a surface and let the child take it with them to spread the word of big and little.

Watch out for little cajun cuisine lovers.
This mixture *is not for consumption* even though it looks good enough to eat.

PAINTING EXPERIENCE #40

OBJECTIVES

Perceptual Motor
Tactile/Kinesthetic Awareness
Fine Motor
Concept Development — colors

CHOICES

MEDIUM (S)	IMPLEMENT (S)	SURFACE (S)
Finger paint — white Liquid hand soap	Rubber gloves — opaque or transparent	Dark construction paper

SUGGESTED DIRECTIONS

Mix the finger paint with a little soap.
I like to give an additional tactile experience by putting some paint into the gloves before the child puts them on.
I also like to tape one paper on the wall for one experience and put another paper on a table or the floor for another experience.
After the child has created with the gloves on, they can remove them and make another creation with their bare hands.

Notes:

I have found that the lightweight transparent gloves are easier for some children to use and you can see what's happening with the paint we put on the inside of the glove. One first grade boy stopped in the middle of his experience and added some red paint to the inside of his glove and giggled as it turned pink but the outside picture remained white.

PAINTING EXPERIENCE #41

OBJECTIVES

Writing Skills
Tactile/Kinesthetic Awareness
Perceptual Motor
Fine Motor
Concept Development — colors, texture, size

CHOICES

MEDIUM (S)	IMPLEMENT (S)	SURFACE (S)
Empty eggs	Hands	Black construction paper
Poster paint — yellow	Baggie	
White glue		
Liquid hand soap		

SUGGESTED DIRECTIONS

You can remove the contents of the eggs by putting a hole in each end and blowing the insides out. Or you can boil the egg and remove the shell in pieces. I prefer to have the whole egg so the child can have the tactile experience of mashing it.

After the shell is broken into little pieces, add the paint and a little soap and some white glue. Scoop the mixture onto the paper and swirl it around. You can put some of the mixture on the paper and use the palm of your hand to smash it down into even finer pieces.

Make a design.

Make a picture.

Make your name.

Notes:

A third grade student used the yellow shells to make egg yokes on his paper.

A tactile defensive kindergarten student with autism very delicately pushed the egg into pieces then took minute little bits and placed them on the paper. The look on his face was twofold. First he looked as if he could not believe anyone would request him to do such a disgusting thing, and secondly that he was actually doing it! He went on to enjoy a good mess!

PAINTING EXPERIENCE #42

OBJECTIVES

Tactile/Kinesthetic Awareness
Perceptual Motor
Fine Motor
Writing Skills
Concept Development — colors, texture

CHOICES

MEDIUM (S)	IMPLEMENT (S)	SURFACE (S)
Glitter — purple	Hands	White construction paper
Finger paints — lavender		
Liquid hand soap		
White school glue		

SUGGESTED DIRECTIONS

Mix the finger paint with the soap and the glue. You have a decision to make. You can either add the glitter now or wait until you have the paint mixture on the surface and sprinkle it on.
If you mix it in, it can get coated with paint and lose the sparkly effect. But it is fun to experiment.
Make a design.
Make a picture.
Make your name.

Notes:

When I was a child I loved glitter, especially gold. To me it was mysterious and very expensive!
I think most children share that view.

PAINTING EXPERIENCE #43

OBJECTIVES

Fun for the dog
Cause and Effect
Concept Development — colors

CHOICES

MEDIUM (S)	IMPLEMENT (S)	SURFACE (S)
Acrylic house paint — red	Small Dog	Painted floor — gray
Liquid hand soap	Paint tray	

SUGGESTED DIRECTIONS

Mix the paint with a little soap. Put a thin layer in the tray. Let the dog walk through the tray and onto the floor. When his paw prints have faded, let him go through the tray again and run around on the floor some more.

Notes:

I really don't expect anyone to try this, but I had to add it, because it is one of my favorite childhood memories.
My aunt had painted her bathroom floor a shiny gray. She was doing the trim red when her pekinese ran through the paint and onto the gray floor. There were little red paw prints everywhere. My aunt picked the dog up and let him run through the red paint again and again until the floor was covered with red paw prints. I wasn't there when my uncle came home from work, but he couldn't have been too mad because the paw prints were still there several years later when my aunt and uncle moved. I always missed that bathroom.

PAINTING EXPERIENCE #44

OBJECTIVES

Tactile/Kinesthetic Awareness
Gross Motor
Concept Development — colors, texture

CHOICES

MEDIUM (S)	IMPLEMENT (S)	SURFACE (S)
Cooked pasta — any shape	Hands	Paper plate
Poster paint — green		
Liquid hand soap		
White school glue		

SUGGESTED DIRECTIONS

Mix the paint and soap with the limp pasta.
Scoop the mixture onto the paper plate. Smash it, swirl it, roll it around.

Notes:

This is going to be the closest you'll come to rolling worms around in paint without being cruel to real worms. I wonder why little kids love that smooshy, gooshy feeling. I have to admit, I kind of do too.
A paper plate is fun to use because it gives a smaller area to work in and has a built in boundary that a piece of paper does not have.

In this age of gummy shapes, go ahead and do gummy worms.
However, have some set aside to eat.

PAINTING EXPERIENCE #45

OBJECTIVES

Tactile/Kinesthetic Awareness
Fine Motor
Perceptual Motor
Writing Skills
Concept Development — color, size

CHOICES

MEDIUM (S)	IMPLEMENT (S)	SURFACE (S)
Poster paint — blue	Big bar of soap	Corrugated cardboard
	Little bar of soap (from motels, trains, etc.)	

SUGGESTED DIRECTIONS

Dip, rub, roll, drag the soap through the paint.
Dip, rub, roll, drag the soap across the cardboard,
Try the big bar of soap.
Try the little bar of soap.
Make a design.
Make a picture.
Make your name.

Notes:

When the soap gets wet it gets slippery and becomes harder to hold onto.
This becomes a challenge and develops those fine motor and adapting skills.
When you are all finished you can wash your hands with the messy soap and watch your hands
and the soap become their original color again.

PAINTING EXPERIENCE #46

OBJECTIVES

Tactile/Kinesthetic Awareness
Fine Motor
Perceptual Motor
Writing Skills
Concept Development — colors

CHOICES

MEDIUM (S)	IMPLEMENT (S)	SURFACE (S)
Poster paint — red, yellow, blue	Plastic fork	White construction paper
	Plastic spoon	
Liquid hand soap	Plastic knife	
Black fine line marker		

SUGGESTED DIRECTIONS

Mix the paint with a little soap.
Trace the knife on the surface with the marker.
Trace the fork on the surface with the marker.
Trace the spoon on the surface with the marker.
Press each utensil in a different color paint and press it onto the matching outline.
Overlap. Drag the utensils on the surface. Drag them, etc.

Notes:

This experience is good for fine motor control because if you push too hard on the utensil it will break. This puts the responsibility of deciding how much pressure to apply on the child.
Do the same experience using cookie cutters.

PAINTING EXPERIENCE #47

OBJECTIVES

Tactile/Kinesthetic Awareness
Fine Motor
Perceptual Motor
Concept Development — colors

CHOICES

MEDIUM (S)	IMPLEMENT (S)	SURFACE (S)
Poster paint — purple	Dried flowers	Pink construction paper
Liquid hand soap		
Green construction paper		
White school glue		

SUGGESTED DIRECTIONS

Mix the paint with a little soap.
Dip or press the flower in the paint. Be careful, they are delicate.
Press it on the paper.
Make a garden.
Cut stems from the green construction paper and glue on the flowers.

Notes:

After we finished the above, we glued dried flowers on another piece of pink construction paper and displayed them side by side.

PLAY EXPERIENCES
21 Experiences

CHOICES FOR PLAY

MEDIUM (S)	IMPLEMENT (S)	SURFACE (S)
darkness	flashlight	room with carpet
tissue paper	hands	air
soap	soap	placemat
snow	body	snow
sand	sponges	sand
paper strips	water toys	paper strips
mud	funnels	mud
water	sieves	body
fake fur	hose	mirror
real fur	fake fur	pool
balloons	real fur	sink
wood	blindfold	bathtub
sandpaper	eyes	table
pasta	sandpaper	sandpaper
beans	spoons	sand table
rice	cups	floor
cornmeal	bowls	trash can
newspaper	pitcher	mouth
gelatin	stove	trash bags
transparent tape	pan	tray
masking tape	knife	paper
shaving cream	feet	hands
pudding	transparent tape	face
aluminum foil	masking tape	
wax paper	shaving cream can	
plastic wrap	baggie	
thin cardboard	paint brush	
tissue paper	instant camera	
water colors	film for camera	
face mask		

PLAY EXPERIENCE #1

OBJECTIVES

Tactile/Kinesthetic Awareness
Body in Space
Visual Awareness

CHOICES

MEDIUM (S)	IMPLEMENT (S)	SURFACE (S)
Darkness	Flashlights	Room with a carpet for those who might tumble

SUGGESTED DIRECTIONS

Pull the blinds. Shut the doors.
Get ready. Turn on your flashlights.
Try to find each other.
Try to find familiar items in the room.
Turn the lights back on. Use the flashlights with the lights on.

Notes:

I have several different flashlights — lantern types, ones with big handles, animal shapes, tiny ones, etc.
It is fun to hang a sheet up and go behind it with your flashlight and take turns putting on a show.

PLAY EXPERIENCE #2

OBJECTIVES

Following Directions
Concept Development — colors, directionality

CHOICES

MEDIUM (S)	IMPLEMENT (S)	SURFACE (S)
Tissue paper — blue, yellow and red	Hands	Air

SUGGESTED DIRECTIONS

Take a piece of tissue paper wide enough to hold with both hands.
Make sure it its long enough to flap in the breeze.
Put it up. Put it down.
Put it on your head. Put it on your neighbor's head.
Put it on the ground and step on it. Jump on it.
Pick it up and make it into a ball.
Take it to the trash can and throw it away.
No, wait!
Go get it and try to throw it into the trash can from your seat.

Notes:

Don't stop where I did. Give as many directions as you can come up with. My students always like to look through the tissue, so we always spend a few minutes doing that.

Also, it is fun to cover all of the windows with a color and have a color day.
Everybody wears that color and every picture made that day is in that color., etc.

PLAY EXPERIENCE #3

OBJECTIVES

Tactile/Kinesthetic Awareness
Concept Development — colors

CHOICES

MEDIUM (S)	IMPLEMENT (S)	SURFACE (S)
Transparent soap bars — red, yellow, blue	Transparent soap bars — red, yellow, blue	Placemats — red, yellow, blue
water	Bowls — red, yellow, blue	
	Small towels — red, yellow, blue	

SUGGESTED DIRECTIONS

Choose a bar of soap. Explore it. What color is it?
Smell it, touch it, look through it, taste it if you want.
Put the red soap in the red bowl.
Set the red bowl on the red placemat.
Do the same with the yellow, then the blue.
Take your favorite soap and wash your hands in the same color bowl.
Dry your hands on the same color towel.

Notes:

Our soap had interesting fragrances. The red was strawberry.
The blue was blueberry and the yellow was lemon.
After looking in many specialty shops for this soap, I finally found it at the local grocery store!

PLAY EXPERIENCE #4

OBJECTIVES

Fine Motor
Tactile/Kinesthetic Awareness

CHOICES

MEDIUM (S)	IMPLEMENT (S)	SURFACE (S)
Newspaper	Hands	Floor
		Trash can or basket

SUGGESTED DIRECTIONS

Put a pile of newspapers on the floor. Start tearing.
Tear fat strips. Tear thin strips. Tear crooked strips.
Throw the strips into a large pile.
Take turns lying down and covering each other up.
Cover only a part of the body or cover the entire body.
Count to three and jump out of the paper pile.
Throw the paper in the air and make paper snow,
Crinkle the paper.

When all finished, pick up every single piece and throw away or save for later.

Notes:

We save our paper strips for use as a collage or for paper mache.
(See Collage Experience #10 or Sculpture Experience #7)

PLAY EXPERIENCE #5

OBJECTIVES

Body Awareness
Tactile/Kinesthetic Awareness
Concept Development — temperature

CHOICES

MEDIUM (S)	IMPLEMENT (S)	SURFACE (S)
Snow	Body —	Snow
Sand	appropriately dressed	Sand
Paper Strips		Paper Strips
Mud		Mud

SUGGESTED DIRECTIONS

Lay on the surface.
Move the arms to the side and above the head. Keep your arms on the surface.
Then return them to your sides.
Move your legs to the side. Keep your legs on the surface.
Bring your legs back together.
Move both arms and legs at the same time.
Stand up carefully and look at your angels.

Notes:

We always play in the snow, sand, etc. for a while before we make our angels. Children tend to calm down and pay more attention if they have had some time to explore first.

PLAY EXPERIENCE #6

OBJECTIVES

Tactile/Kinesthetic Awareness
Concept Development — body parts

CHOICES

MEDIUM (S)	IMPLEMENT (S)	SURFACE (S)
Warm water	Sponges — all sizes	Body Mirror

SUGGESTED DIRECTIONS

Identify each other's body parts with a wet sponge.
Sit in front of a mirror and identify your own body parts.
Identify them on the mirror.

Notes:

Children enjoy being in charge and doing things to others in a constructive manner.
They can be very gentle with each other.

PLAY EXPERIENCE #7

OBJECTIVES

Tactile/Kinesthetic Awareness
Gross Motor
Fine Motor

CHOICES

MEDIUM (S)	IMPLEMENT (S)	SURFACE (S)
Water	Body	Pool, sink, bath tub
	Water toys — funnels, sieves, etc.	

SUGGESTED DIRECTIONS

Be limited only by the amount of water you have.

Notes:

Our staff brings in their assorted sprinklers and hoses and we play with these. Also, little pools are easy to transport from one place to another.

Of course, we have appropriate clothing on hand — swim suits, towels, etc.
This is a good time to practice dressing skills.

PLAY EXPERIENCE #8

OBJECTIVES

Tactile/Kinesthetic Awareness
Concept Development — body parts

CHOICES

MEDIUM (S)	IMPLEMENT (S)	SURFACE (S)
Fake fur — short nap and long nap	Fake fur	Body
Real fur	Real fur	

SUGGESTED DIRECTIONS

Pass the fur around. Feel it. Smell it.
Rub it on your face, your arms, your legs, etc.
Toss it in the air and catch.
Get it wet. How does it feel?
Brush it. Comb it.

Notes:

I have a collection of old fur coats. I usually have them shortened so I have several inches of real fur. I let the children play with this. I have several different textures from long and silky to short and stubby. The favorites are a horse hide and a polar bear.
If you can pet real animals at the same time, it is fun to compare.

Animal's rights people: I said _OLD_ fur coats — antiques.

PLAY EXPERIENCE #9

OBJECTIVES

Body in Space

CHOICES

MEDIUM (S)	IMPLEMENT (S)	SURFACE (S)
Balloons	Body	Room

SUGGESTED DIRECTIONS

Blow up the balloons.
Make sure there aren't obstacles where you choose to play.
Start batting and blowing.
Try to keep the balloons moving.

Notes:

One Halloween we were given over a hundred orange and black balloons. We had an empty room across the hall, so we blew up the balloons and put the balloons and the children together in the empty room. It was constant directed motion. There were fifteen children with autism and four children in wheelchairs. We played for over an hour. Even when the balloons hit the floor they would not stay still.

Water balloons can also be fun, but there isn't the same tranquil atmosphere.

PLAY EXPERIENCE #10

OBJECTIVES

Tactile/Kinesthetic Awareness
Visual Awareness
Concept Development — texture

CHOICES

MEDIUM (S)	IMPLEMENT (S)	SURFACE (S)
Block of rough wood	Hands	Table
Sandpaper — all grades two of each	Eyes	
	blindfold	
	Sandpaper — all grades	

SUGGESTED DIRECTIONS

Feel the sandpaper. Rub lightly over face, hands, arms, etc.
Sand the wood until it is smooth.
Blindfold and try to match fine sandpaper with fine, medium with medium, etc.

Notes:

Watch closely that children don't rub too hard on their skin.

Make sandpaper letters and numbers and glue down.
Make sandpaper shapes and glue down.

PLAY EXPERIENCE #11

OBJECTIVES

Tactile/Kinesthetic Awareness
Concept Development — shapes

CHOICES

MEDIUM (S)	IMPLEMENT (S)	SURFACE (S)
Pasta — all shapes wheels, shells, spaghetti, etc. cooked and cooled	Hands	Table

SUGGESTED DIRECTIONS

Take the cooled pasta and do anything your little heart desires.
Squish it. Smash it. Try to stack it. You can even eat it.
Arrange it and let it dry.

Notes:

Cooked pasta is as much fun as playing in the mud!

If you get really adventurous you can squish it with your feet. Pretend you are making pasta wine.

PLAY EXPERIENCE #12

OBJECTIVES

Fine Motor
Tactile/Kinesthetic Awareness
Concept Development — size, texture

CHOICES

MEDIUM (S)	IMPLEMENT (S)	SURFACE (S)
Beans	Hands	Sand table or similar
Rice	Spoons	
Cornmeal	Cups	
Sand	Bowls, etc.	
Uncooked Pasta – all shapes		

SUGGESTED DIRECTIONS

Put one of the above or a combination in a sand table.
Sift, measure, pour, etc.

Notes:

This activity provides self initiated play time.
It is as soothing as watching the ocean waves come and go.

PLAY EXPERIENCE #13

OBJECTIVES

Fine Motor

CHOICES

MEDIUM (S)	IMPLEMENT (S)	SURFACE (S)
Water	Pitcher	Sink
Rice		Container
Sand		

SUGGESTED DIRECTIONS

Fill pitcher with water and practice pouring all of the water into the sink.

Fill the pitcher with water and practice pouring into a large glass.
Practice pouring into smaller glasses.

Repeat the procedure using rice, using sand.
(Don't pour these into the sink, but your can pour them into a dish pan.)

Notes:

Pouring seems to be one of those universal experiences that all kids love to do.

PLAY EXPERIENCE #14

OBJECTIVES

Tactile/Kinesthetic Awareness
Concept Development — temperature

CHOICES

MEDIUM (S)	IMPLEMENT (S)	SURFACE (S)
4 envelopes unflavored gelatine	Bowl, knife, spoon, stove, pan.	Mouth
1 1/2 cups cold fruit juice		Table
1 1/2 cups boiling fruit juice		

SUGGESTED DIRECTIONS

Sprinkle unflavored gelatin over cold juice and let it stand for one minute.
Add hot juice and stir until gelatin is dissolved.
Pour in shallow pan and chill until firm.
Cut into shapes.
Pick up, look through, wobble, stack, eat.

Notes:

Scrub everyone's hands before beginning, and wash the table down. There's nothing worse than watching hairy gelatin disappear down a child's throat.
Use cookie cutters to make interesting shapes.

Push the blocks through a food grater to make interesting noodle shapes.
I have an antique food grinder that we put our gelatin through and it looked a lot like gummy worms coming out.

PLAY EXPERIENCE #15

OBJECTIVES

Tactile/Kinesthetic Awareness
Concept Development — colors, temperature

CHOICES

MEDIUM (S)	IMPLEMENT (S)	SURFACE (S)
Gelatin — any color	Feet	Large shallow tray
Water		or garbage bag

SUGGESTED DIRECTIONS

Mix gelatin according to directions on package.
Refrigerate until semi firm.
Spread gelatin out on surface.
Take off shoes and socks.
Walk through the gelatin.
Stop and squish your toes.
Walk out of gelatin and into water to clean feet.

Notes:

We had large pieces of paper at the end of the walk and made footprints on the paper. It made a pretty wall hanging for the classroom.

Have someone posted on either side of the gelatin walker as it is very slippery.

PLAY EXPERIENCE #16

OBJECTIVES

Tactile/Kinesthetic Awareness
Fine Motor

CHOICES

MEDIUM (S)	IMPLEMENT (S)	SURFACE (S)
Transparent tape in holder	Transparent tape in holder	Paper
Masking tape	Masking tape	Hands

SUGGESTED DIRECTIONS

Tear off a piece of either type of tape at least a foot long.
Try to make a person, an animal, a shape.
Tape pieces of paper together.
Tape tape together.
Play catch with tape balls.
Roll them on the floor.
Pick up other objects with the tape.

Notes:

We started playing with tape after I would ask children to pull tape off the display board and throw it away. They were reluctant to throw it away. They would try to take the longest time possible to get to the trash can while twisting and pulling on the tape.

PLAY EXPERIENCE #17

OBJECTIVES

Tactile/Kinesthetic Awareness
Concept Development — body parts

CHOICES

MEDIUM (S)	IMPLEMENT (S)	SURFACE (S)
Shaving cream — white or the kind that turns green after it's rubbed around	Shaving cream can	Body

SUGGESTED DIRECTIONS

Put on bathing suits or old clothes.
Squirt shaving cream on each other.
Identify body parts with shaving cream.
Squirt shaving cream on the floor or ground and slide in it.
March in it! Dance in it!

Notes:

I like to throw in a can of magic string that doesn't squirt shaving cream although it looks like it will. It just shoots out string.

PLAY EXPERIENCE #18

OBJECTIVES

Tactile/Kinesthetic Awareness
Concept Development — temperature, texture

CHOICES

MEDIUM (S)	IMPLEMENT (S)	SURFACE (S)
Water — hot and cold	Baggie — Zip-Lock	Table top or floor
mud		
gelatin		
sand		
pudding		
shaving cream, etc.		

SUGGESTED DIRECTIONS

Fill a bag with hot water and seal it. Fill a bag with cold water and seal it. Fill a bag with mud and seal it, etc.
Put bags on a table. Choose one and squeeze it, roll it, toss it.
Talk about it.

Notes:

Have lots of paper towels for clean up when one of the bags bursts, because they will. Then it becomes a whole new sensory experience. We dump the contents out when we are finished and feel it outside of the bag. This experience is good for concept exploration. Hot, cold. Rough, smooth, etc.

PLAY EXPERIENCE #19

OBJECTIVES

Tactile/Kinesthetic Awareness
Concept Development — body parts

CHOICES

MEDIUM (S)	IMPLEMENT (S)	SURFACE (S)
Water colors in a tray	Paint brush	Face
Liquid hand soap	Instant camera	
	Mirror	

SUGGESTED DIRECTIONS

Mix the paint with a little soap.
Look in the mirror as you paint your face. Photograph the process.
Watch the pictures develop.
Wash your face.
Paint someone else or just watch.

Notes:

The tickling of the paint brush is a fun side benefit from this experience.
Tickle the face with the dry brush before beginning.
Animal faces seem to be our favorite. Maybe it is the whiskers.

PLAY EXPERIENCE #20

OBJECTIVES

Tactile/Kinesthetic Awareness
Concept Development — body parts
Speech and Language

CHOICES

MEDIUM (S)	IMPLEMENT (S)	SURFACE (S)
Mild face mask	Hands	Face
	Instant Camera	

SUGGESTED DIRECTIONS

Spread the mask over the face. Let dry.
Don't laugh. . . Don't frown. . . Don't cry.
Photograph the process.
When good and dry, rinse off. Move your face around.

Notes:

Always check for allergic reactions before beginning this experience.
This experience always seems to bring the "ham" out in children.
Use photographs for speech and language lessons.

PLAY EXPERIENCE #21

OBJECTIVES

Tactile/Kinesthetic Awareness

CHOICES

MEDIUM (S)	IMPLEMENT (S)	SURFACE (S)
Aluminum foil	Hands	Table
Wax paper	Eyes	
Plastic wrap	Blindfold	
Thin cardboard		
Tissue paper		

SUGGESTED DIRECTIONS

Take a piece of aluminum foil and scrunch it up in a ball.
Flatten it out. What happened?
Do the same with the other mediums.
Put blindfold on and try to identify the mediums.
With blindfold on, listen to the sound each medium makes as you scrunch it,
tear it, fold it, wave it, etc.

Notes:

Save all the scrunched up mediums for a collage.
(See Collage Experience #8.)

SCULPTURE EXPERIENCES
10 Experiences

CHOICES FOR SCULPTURE EXPERIENCES

MEDIUM (S)	IMPLEMENT (S)	SURFACE (S)
string	hands	balloon
white flour	bowl	sand
water	pitcher	styrofoam shapes
plaster of paris	paper clip	baby food jars
self-hardening clay	tablespoon	
feathers	teaspoon	
sand	baby spoon	
newspaper	strong glue	
poster paint	spray starch	
rolls —	needle	
paper towel	thread	
toilet tissue		
wrapping paper		
carpet, etc.		
bar soap		
lace		
panty hose		
stuffing		

SCULPTURE EXPERIENCE #1

OBJECTIVES

Tactile/Kinesthetic Awareness
Fine Motor
Perceptual Motor
Concept Development — size

CHOICES

MEDIUM (S)	IMPLEMENT (S)	SURFACE (S)
Rolls — all sizes paper towel, toilet paper, wrapping paper, carpet, etc.	Strong glue	

SUGGESTED DIRECTIONS

Start glueing rolls to rolls in any way or shape imaginable.
Do it individually or as a group project.

Notes:

A first grader decided to make a "juk castle", (his pronounciation). He brought in a cardboard box, rolls of all sizes, contact paper, net guttering, shoe boxes, and fabric softener boxes (for jails inside the castle). He turned out quite an elaborate castle. It was a present for me and it still sits in my basement.

You can also do the above experience with paper cups instead of rolls or a combination of both.

SCULPTURE EXPERIENCE #2

OBJECTIVES

Tactile/Kinesthetic Awareness
Fine Motor
Perceptual Motor
Concept Development — body parts, texture

CHOICES

MEDIUM (S)	IMPLEMENT (S)	SURFACE (S)
Plaster of paris	Pitcher	Sand in a box or shallow tray
Water	Hand	
	Paper clip	

SUGGESTED DIRECTIONS

Get the sand damp. Press your hand into the clay.
Make sure it has made a deep enough impression.
Mix the plaster of paris with the water according to the directions on the box. You can mix it right in the pitcher.
Pour into the hand impression.
Bend a paper clip and stick into the wet plaster for hanging later.
Let dry.

Notes:

You can paint these if you wish, but we like the stark simplicity of the white.
We have also done our feet.
You can press objects into the sand and pour plaster into the impressions.
A group of children (with autism, cerebral palsy, mental retardation, and visual and hearing impairments) helped me fill a rubber glove with plaster. We all felt it and squeezed it, etc. After it dried, we cut the glove off and had a hand. We counted its fingers, shook it and painted its fingernails.

If a child will sit still long enough, you can pour the plaster directly into their hand and let them feel the temperature changes it goes through and feel it harden in their hand. This makes a nice paper weight.

SCULPTURE EXPERIENCE #3

OBJECTIVES

Tactile/Kinesthetic Awareness
Fine Motor
Perceptual Motor
Concept Development — colors, texture

CHOICES

MEDIUM (S)	IMPLEMENT (S)	SURFACE (S)
Feathers — all colors	Hands	Styrofoam shape

SUGGESTED DIRECTIONS

Stick the feathers into the styrofoam shape until it is covered.

Notes:

You can buy the feathers at a craft shop.
We take a long hat pin with the "T" top and stick it in the shape so a string can be attached to it and the shape can be hung up.

We tickle each other with these and they are great to put in feely boxes.

SCULPTURE EXPERIENCE #4

OBJECTIVES

Tactile/Kinesthetic Awareness
Fine Motor

CHOICES

MEDIUM (S)	IMPLEMENT (S)	SURFACE (S)
Panty hose material	Needle	
Stuffing	Thread	

SUGGESTED DIRECTIONS

Cut the foot off a pair of panty hose.
Stuff it tightly.
Sew the end up.
Using the needle and thread, create a face.

Using smaller pieces of panty hose, make arms and legs and sew them on.

Notes:

Since this is known as soft sculpture, I thought I would include it in my sculpture section. I loved making dolls when I was a child. I really felt like I had made something.

SCULPTURE EXPERIENCE #5

OBJECTIVES

Tactile/Kinesthetic Awareness
Fine Motor
Concept Development — texture

CHOICES

MEDIUM (S)	IMPLEMENT (S)	SURFACE (S)
Lace	Spray starch	

SUGGESTED DIRECTIONS

Drape the cloth over a bottle or other stationary shape.
Spray it with the starch and let dry. Spray it again and again, at least five times, letting it dry between each spraying. Be careful not to move it until you are finished.

Notes:

These stiff pieces of lace make pretty window decorations and are also pretty as holiday decorations.

Use the same process with tissue paper over a bottle and it becomes a ghost when dry.

SCULPTURE EXPERIENCE #6

OBJECTIVES

Tactile/Kinesthetic Awareness
Fine Motor

CHOICES

MEDIUM (S)	IMPLEMENT (S)	SURFACE (S)
Bar soap	Hands	
Water		

SUGGESTED DIRECTIONS

Cut the soap into small chunks and some larger chunks. Soak them in water.
When it is nice and gooey, mold the chunks into shapes and stick together.
Make a person.
Make a shape.
Make your name.

When it dries, it can be your very own, personal soap.

Notes:

This is another good activity for tactile defensive children. The slimy soap really has a strange
feel to it that isn't all that unpleasant. It is just different.

SCULPTURE EXPERIENCE #7

OBJECTIVES

Tactile/Kinesthetic Awareness
Fine Motor
Perceptual Motor
Concept Development — colors, texture

CHOICES

MEDIUM (S)	IMPLEMENT (S)	SURFACE (S)
Newspaper strips	Hands	Balloon
White flour	Bowl	
Water		
Poster paint — your choice		

SUGGESTED DIRECTIONS

Blow up the balloon and secure the end.
Mix the flour with water until it is the consistency of gravy.
The strips are easier to work with if they are about 1" or 2" wide and about a foot long.
Dip the strips, one at a time, into the gravy. As you pull the strip out, run two fingers down the front and back of the strip removing excess paste.
Wrap the strip around the balloon and smooth it down. Repeat until the balloon is covered with a light layer. Let it dry and repeat the process. When you are all finished, you can either pop the balloon with a pin or let it wither away all by itself.

Decide what you are going to make out of your shape and paint it.

Notes:

We have made heads from our balloons and put yarn on for hair.
Another thing we have done is to put the balloon on a stick and paint the balloon a bright color. Put it with several other paper mache balloons, and we have a permanent balloon collection to decorate the room with. A good activity for circus time. Also, you can leave the stick off and hang a grouping of balloons form the ceiling.
My third grade class made a zoo using paper mache. We use cans of all sizes for feet. Legs were made of various sized rolls. We used coat hangers to form ears. Then we coated the animals with paper mache. When they were dry, we covered them with tissue paper (all colors) and coated them with white glue and water. I made an elephant that you can read about in the January, 1977, issue of *Arts and Activities.* The article is entitled, "Build a Baby Elephant".
    (See PLAY EXPERIENCE #4, pp. 92)

SCULPTURE EXPERIENCE #8

OBJECTIVES

Tactile/Kinesthetic Awareness
Fine Motor
Perceptual Motor
Concept Development — color, texture

CHOICES

MEDIUM (S)	IMPLEMENT (S)	SURFACE (S)
Sand — blue, yellow, red	Tablespoon	Baby food jars
	Teaspoon	
	Tiny baby spoon	

SUGGESTED DIRECTIONS

Make sure the baby food jars are sparkling clean.
Put a layer of red in the bottom of the jar. Push it up the sides a little.
Add a layer of yellow. Careful not to mix the two colors.
Now add a layer of blue. Repeat until the jar is full.
Put the lid on and set it someplace and admire it.

Use the tablespoon with children that need work on fine motor skills, and let them work towards using the baby spoon.

Notes:

You can spray paint the lid to make it more attractive, or cover it with a piece of material with a rubber band around it, or just glue a piece of construction paper on it.

Although I discourage shaking, it is okay if it happens. A whole new look appears.

I let the children play in the sand before we begin without mixing it up, of course. This is a good experience to follow regular sand play instead of letting the children play in the colored sand. They do get a little overzealous in the sand and you won't have to worry about all the pretty sand ending up on the floor.

SCULPTURE EXPERIENCE #9

OBJECTIVES

Tactile/Kinesthetic Awareness
Fine Motor
Perceptual Motor
Concept Development — texture

CHOICES

MEDIUM (S)	IMPLEMENT (S)	SURFACE (S)
Self-hardening clay	Hands	

SUGGESTED DIRECTIONS

Squeeze, pound, roll, etc. the clay into any shape you want.
Let it dry.

Notes:

It does not matter what you make out of the clay, because it is so fascinating to leave it wet and come back and it is dry and hard.

SCULPTURE EXPERIENCE #10

OBJECTIVES

Tactile/Kinesthetic Awareness
Fine Motor
Perceptual Motor
Concept Development — texture

CHOICES

MEDIUM (S)	IMPLEMENT (S)	SURFACE (S)
String	Hands	Balloon
White flour	Bowl	
Water		

SUGGESTED DIRECTIONS

Blow up the balloon and secure the end.
Mix the flour with water until it is the consistency of gravy.
The string is easier to work with if it is about one foot long.
Dip a piece of string into the gravy. As you pull the string out, run two fingers down the string to re-move excess paste.
Wrap the string around the balloon and smooth it down.
Repeat until you have an interesting criss-cross pattern covering the entire balloon.
When the string is dry, take a pin and pop the balloon and pull it out.

Notes:

If you use very small balloons, they can be used for holiday ornaments.
You can paint these if you like, but I think the natural color of the string is nice.